SEA HARR

AEROGUIDE 32: BAe SEA HARRIER FRS Mk 1/FA Mk 2

Roger Chesneau

AD HOC PUBLICATIONS

INTRODUCTION

A T FIRST acclaimed as, and subsequently proven to be, the world's most effective all-round naval combat aircraft of the last quarter of the twentieth century, the Sea Harrier represented a concept that had long been discussed but took some considerable time to put into practice—the operation of fixed-wing V/STOL (Vertical/Short Take-Off and Landing) combat aircraft from warships. After World War II, carrier aviation witnessed revolutionary changes as ships were forced up to unprecedented dimensions in order to cope with ever faster and heavier aircraft and compelled to install more and more powerful catapults and sophisticated arresting gear so as to launch and recover them safely. The attraction of minimum-area flight decks from which aircraft could rise vertically and to which they might return in similar mode finally proved irresistible with the phasing out of the last of the Royal Navy's conventional carriers in 1978.

As these words are written (March 2006), the Royal Navy's Sea Harrier force is reduced to one squadron, and it is due to be disbanded totally within a matter of weeks. Thus the Fleet Air Arm—not for the first time in its history—finds itself emasculated, lacking a dedicated air defence capability until at least 2012. This is when the first of a pair of new fleet carriers is scheduled to come into service; FAA fixed-wing squadrons are then supposed to recommission with the STOVL (Short Take-Off and Vertical Landing) version of the F-35 Joint Strike Fighter (JSF), although it remains to be seen whether this will be a trouble-free procurement. In the interim, '. . . we don't fight the kind of wars where our ships need defending from enemy warplanes far out at sea,' said a British Government minister in 2002. 'If necessary, we can

Below: A Sea Harrier FRS.1 from 700A Flight—the Intensive Flying Trials Unit based at RNAS Yeovilton— hovers alongside HMS *Invincible*, 1979.

rely on coalition forces to provide the outer air defence for surface ships.'(!) This perfectly illustrates the level of political commitment to the Defence of the Realm in 2006.

The Sea Harrier's place in aviation history is, however, assured, if only for its outstanding contribution to the recapture of the Falkland Islands in the 1982 South Atlantic War between Britain and Argentina. Indeed, the aircraft can lay claim to being the single most important factor in the victory, accounting as it did for nearly two dozen enemy aircraft; four 'kills' on the first day of the air war represented a huge psychological message and established an advantage that was never lost.

This *Aeroguide* is a completely revised, updated and very much enlarged edition of one of the first books in the series, number 3, which was first published in 1983, and once again features in its close-up photography the aircraft—now FA Mk 2s as well as FRS Mk 1s—of 899 Naval Air Squadron. For assistance, advice and permissions, the author and publishers would like to express their thanks to OC RNAS Yeovilton and OC 899 NAS; to former personnel of 899 NAS, especially CPO AEM Dean Harpham and LAEM Kevin Musgrove; to BAe Systems, especially Barry Guess and Mike Fielding; to Dick Ward; to Del Holyland and the Martin-Baker Aircraft Company; to Ray Rimell; and to Diego Bigolin, Howard Cargill, Kristof Jonckheere, Neil Jones, H. B. Kannan, Mark McEwan, Charles Polidano and Simon Watson.   R.D.C.

ROYAL NAVY/COURTESY RICHARD L. WARD

EVOLUTION

THE INTRODUCTORY remarks made at the beginning of this book referred to the Sea Harrier's place in aviation history owing to its considerable achievements during the course of the 1982 Falklands War, but the aircraft represents a milestone in another, altogether different way: it is, and is likely forever to remain, the last British fighter aircraft of wholly indigenous design to have been produced specifically for that role. As such, it is also the final issue in a huge family of fighter aircraft—almost without exception successful aircraft—that can trace its ancestry back to the Sopwith Aviation Company, which produced the immortal Camel, Pup and Snipe fighters of World War I. Thus, when the Sea Harrier bows out of service in 2006, an extraordinary lineage will be extinguished.

Hawker Aircraft—the *alter ego* of Sopwith Aviation on that company's dissolution in 1920—was indisputably the most successful manufacturer of fighter and trainer aircraft in Great Britain (and, arguably, in the world) during its tenure at Kingston-upon-Thames in Surrey, responsible for an unbroken line of first-rate equipment for use by the Royal Air Force and to a lesser extent by the Fleet Air Arm, and in most instances for export too. By and large, the successive designs emanating from the Kingston design offices were for conventional, straight-forward aircraft, each building on the accumulated experience gained and incorporating proven new technology where appropriate. The Hawker company's Project 1127, however, first mooted in 1957, was, to put it mildly, radical.

The postwar years were littered with proposals and designs for military aircraft that would require no runway, thus enabling them to operate from locations that would be difficult to pinpoint by an enemy. Several succeeded inasmuch as they progressed beyond the drawing board, but these all demonstrated severe limitations, not least because their thrust-over-weight superiority, while enabling the aircraft to fly, was too marginal or their engine arrangement too

Below (clockwise from top left): XP980, one of the four DB (Development Batch) Hawker P.1127s; an RAF Harrier GR.1, the first production variant in the Harrier family; a Sea Harrier FRS.51 — for the Indian Navy — on flight trials and in primer finish; XZ451, the first Sea Harrier to be delivered to the Fleet Air Arm; a production Sea Harrier FRS.1 in the markings of 899 Naval Air Squadron; and a Sea Harrier FRS Mk 2 (later to be designated FA Mk 2) on a flight test and fitted with 190-gallon long-range tanks and four AMRAAMs.

complex to permit them to do much else (for example, manoeuvre, or carry a useful load). It was not until the advent of vectored thrust — proposed in a sketch design by the Frenchman Michel Wibault — that a practical VTOL aircraft seemed a real possibility. To cut a fascinating story to the bone, Wibault discussed his ideas with Stanley Hooker, Technical Director of Bristol Aero Engines, which company's Project Engineer Gordon Lewis transformed the theory into the BE.52 engine, which, refined into the BE.53, was later dubbed the Pegasus; in the meantime Hawker's Chief Engineer, Sir Sydney Camm, was introduced to Hooker's ideas and passed them to his Future Designs team at Kingston. The betrothal culminated in a marriage, and Project 1127 was conceived.

The early 1960s were a time of huge upheaval for the British aircraft industry: the shock waves generated by Duncan Sandys' 1957 Defence White Paper, which declared that the RAF would in the future require neither manned interceptors nor manned bombers (although it did *not* decree, as many believe, that no offensive aircraft would henceforth be produced for the Services), still had not dissipated, and in this political atmosphere it was something of a miracle that the P.1127 survived to spawn a family of aircraft that went on to enjoy huge success and is still, to this day, unique in concept.

SEA HARRIER MARK ONE

The front-line aircraft that evolved from the P.1127 — the RAF's Harrier GR.1 — entered service on 1 April 1969. It was a very different aircraft from the P.1127, although the family resemblance was plain enough. It was about this time that studies for a dedicated shipborne version began to gather momentum at Kingston: the fact that the Royal Navy's fleet aircraft carriers had received the death sentence from the British Government some three years earlier was of

Above: A pristine Sea Harrier FRS.1 within the hangar aboard HMS *Invincible*. One of the ship's 'scissors' lifts can be glimpsed in the background.

course not coincidental. The impetus was generated by the prospect of combat jets flying from helicopter carriers, assault ships, helicopter cruisers—indeed, any sort of vessel that could accommodate a landing platform; neither was the potential overlooked for such an aircraft in the export market, where navies with smaller budgets might for the first time in their histories be able to operate a seaborne air arm with a serious offensive capability.

The existing Harrier, the RAF's GR Mk 1, was essentially a 'mud-mover'—a ground-attack aircraft tasked with such roles as the close air support of armoured and infantry divisions. A shipboard variant would at the very least require an air defence capability, calling for the carriage of air-to-air missiles and a radar suite to locate and hunt down intruding aircraft; further refinements would include a raised cockpit position, affording the pilot a view 'over-the-shoulder' more in keeping with the requirements of a fighter aircraft; the substitution of aluminium components (principally in the Pegasus engine) for magnesium, which is less prone to corrosion in a salt-laden environment; and the replacement of various electronics systems and cockpit instruments with equipment more appropriate to the naval role. The twin 30mm Aden cannon of the RAF Harrier were retained, but an anti-ship capability was introduced with the addition of circuitry for a pair of Sea Eagle missiles. The radar nose housed Ferranti Blue Fox, derived from the existing Sea Spray system already installed in the Navy's Lynx helicopters, and a Decca Doppler radar and twin-gyro platform was selected in place of the original Harrier's INS (which would have been difficult, or expensive, to calibrate in a seaway).

SKI-JUMP TO SUCCESS

It was fully understood from the beginning of the Harrier programme that vertical take-off (VTO), whilst a useful resource, was hardly conducive to maximum effectiveness in terms of the aircraft's weapons carriage (or, with fuel tanks fitted, its range): a rolling take-off, even a short one, enabled a much greater load to be taken into the air, since lift would then be generated by the flying surfaces as well as merely by the downthrust of the engine. Taking this principal a stage further, by increasing the angle of attack of the aircraft during take-off, the run required would be cut yet further—of particular interest where flight-deck space was at a premium (for example, in a light aircraft carrier), and of course already practised in fleet carriers, where aircraft were commonly launched tail-down from catapults.

Thus was born the famous 'ski-jump'—a ramp, concave in profile, which enabled the aircraft to leave the flight deck in a pitched-up attitude. The whole point of the ramp was not to imbue the aircraft with greater speed, as is often thought: it was to buy time, since an aircraft on an upward trajectory has many more seconds available in which to attain the required forward airspeed to facilitate wing-generated lift. By no means incidentally, it also gave the pilot more time to eject in the event of an aircraft malfunction. Trials were conducted at the Royal Aircraft

Right: An FRS.1 equipped with dummy Sea Eagle anti-ship missiles leaves the 'ski-jump' test platform at RAE Bedford.

Right: FRS.1 ZA174, yet to receive its final paint scheme, on a test flight from Dunsfold, September 1981.

NOT PROCEEDED WITH

The unique capabilities of the Harrier seemed, for a while, to offer unique possibilities for deploying combat aircraft at sea, and several design studies were initiated to this end. One such was SkyHook, investigated as a joint venture by British Aerospace and Dowty Boulton Paul in the early 1980s. The system envisaged the launch and capture of Sea Harriers by means of auto-stabilised, sensor-equipped shipboard cranes. Launch would

of course require the aircraft to run up its engine until free hover could be achieved, whereupon the crane jack would release; in recovery, the pilot would align his aircraft with a 'hover sight' and the jack on the crane would lock on to a contact probe fitted in the upper panelling of the aircraft's fuselage. The aircraft would then be swung into its hangar, where it could if necessary be replenished, rearmed and re-launched.

Trials were conducted on land using a specially modified fire engine turntable and indeed showed considerable promise, but interest died and the project was abandoned.

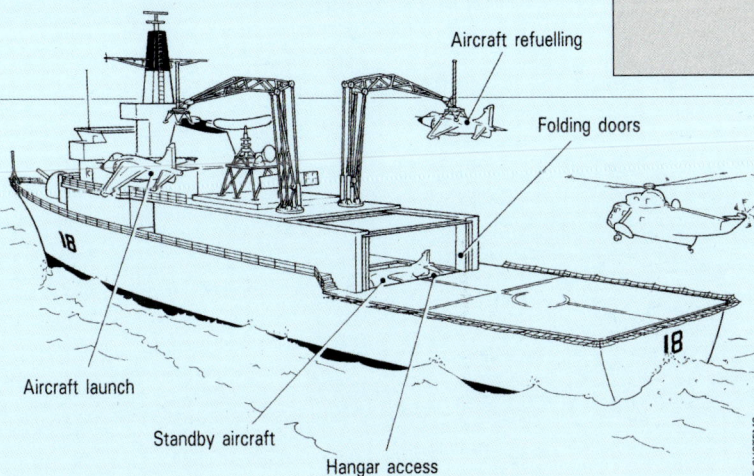

Aircraft refuelling

Folding doors

Aircraft launch

Standby aircraft

Hangar access

Establishment at Bedford, where it was demonstrated that, given a steep enough angle (15–20 degrees), the take-off run could be reduced by 60 per cent or, alternatively, the aircraft's warload could be increased by some 30 per cent.

TO SEA

An order for two dozen Sea Harriers was formally placed by HM Government in May 1975, but it would be over three years before the first example, XZ450, was flown. There were no prototypes in the traditional sense: the aircraft's commonality with the RAF's Harrier was deemed sufficient to render these superfluous. At around the time of the maiden flight, August 1978, it was announced that a further ten aircraft were to be built; however, by the time production was halted a total of 57 had been built for the RN.

The practicalities of operating V/STOL (Vertical/Short Take-Off and Landing) fixed-wing air-craft from shipboard platforms had been investigated early in the pre-Harrier programme, when on 8 February 1963 the first P.1127, XP831, had carried out preliminary compatibility trials on board *Ark Royal*. Shipboard trials of the Sea Harrier proper were carried out in November 1979, after the first few aircraft had been handed over to the Fleet Air Arm and the first squadron commissioned. The operational advantages of the 'ski-jump' had meanwhile proved irresistible, and, as a result, the light aircraft carriers earmarked to host the Sea Harrier squadrons—the three erstwhile 'through-deck cruisers' of the *Invincible* class—were hastily modified to

Above: HMS *Invincible* at sea, with a lone Sea Harrier FRS.1 aft preparing to conduct compatibility trials. Left: Pre-production Sea Harrier XZ438 on board HMS *Hermes* for trials. The unique tail code presumably denotes the fact that this aircraft was operated by the Ministry of Defence rather than an FAA unit.

Left: Press Day aboard *Invincible*, with a Sea Harrier of 801 Naval Air squadron demonstrating for the cameras, June 1981.

Above right: Crew and air group topside, a smart looking *Hermes* makes gentle way, Portsmouth, early 1982.
Below: A sombre-looking 800 NAS Sea Harrier aboard *Hermes* in 1983.

incorporate a launch ramp over the bows; as an interim measure pending their completion, the commando carrier *Hermes*, herself formerly a conventional light fleet carrier, was refitted in a similar manner. *Invincible* and *Illustrious* were fitted with 7-degree ramps while the new *Ark Royal* and *Hermes* were equipped with ramps of 12 degrees.

These vessels could not, of course, be compared with the fleet aircraft carriers of the 1950s and 1960s, which could accommodate an air group of some three to four dozen fixed-wing aircraft; even *Hermes* could take up to thirty in her heyday. Although they have room for, and indeed have embarked, larger numbers, the original complement of the *Invincible*s was nine Sea King helicopters and a mere five Sea Harriers.

EXPORT

PRODIGIOUS efforts by the manufacturers notwithstanding, the Sea Harrier has, it has to be said, proved something of a disappointment in terms of its export sales: the only customer has been the Indian Navy. Hopes were entertained also of supplying at least the Spanish and Italian Navies, which in the early 1980s were planning air groups for their new light aircraft carriers, but in the event a version of the US-inspired AV-8B Harrier was bought instead. The combat record of the Sea Harrier, recently proven in the South Atlantic, unfortunately did not sway political minds.

The Indian Navy was, however, suitably impressed, and ordered the aircraft virtually 'off the drawing board', six aircraft (designated FRS Mk 51) and two trainers being ordered in November 1979. Follow-up orders were forthcoming for seventeen and two aircraft, respectively, in two batches, while replacements for attritional losses have also been delivered. The Indian aircraft—all of which are assigned to No 300 Squadron—were originally deployed aboard the carrier *Vikrant* but are currently (2006) operated from that ship's replacement, the *Viraat* (formerly the British carrier *Hermes*, of Falklands War fame).

The expansion of the Indian Navy, one aspect of which is its purchase of the former Soviet aircraft carrier *Admiral Gorshkov* and another the construction of an indigenous 'air defence ship' to be commissioned *circa* 2008, led to a British proposal in February 2006 to supply surplus Sea Harrier FA.2s to the Indian Navy, but it is not known at the time of writing whether this offer will be taken up.

This spread: Indian Navy Sea Harriers under test (right) and in service with No 300 Squadron. The first Mk 51 was officially handed over in January 1983. Initially deployed aboard *Vikrant* (a British *Majestic* class light fleet carrier), the aircraft now operate from *Viraat* (the former HMS *Hermes*). No 300 Squadron's white tiger emblem is evident on some of the aircraft, which have also seen a toning down of their colour scheme over the years—and are, it is reported, currently being upgraded with the installation of Israeli EL/M-2032 radar and the Rafael Derby AAM.

SIMON WATSON

B. HARRY/ACIG.org

BAE SYSTEMS

B. HARRY/ACIG.org

SIMON WATSON

COMBAT

A QUARTER of a century ago, in the distant waters of the South Atlantic Ocean, the 'Black Death' reigned supreme. However, this was no medieval-style epidemic: it was the sobriquet accorded the Sea Harrier by Argentine pilots, who suffered considerable losses at its hands. *La Muerta Negra*, as the Argentines called it, flew every type of mission in keeping with its designation—fighter, reconnaissance and strike—and fully justified the investment that had been made in it.

The story of Operation 'Corporate'—the retaking of the Falkland Islands between April and June 1982 following their seizure by the Argentines—is well known, has been copiously written up in numerous publications and will not be dwelt upon here. As far as the Sea Harriers were concerned, it was a conflict in which the aircraft's critics were confounded, in which a handful of brave pilots and a body of incredibly hard-working and dedicated maintenance crews performed heroics, in which the reliability of both engine and avionics exceeded expectations by a very wide margin, and in which the aircraft taking part suffered not a single loss in air combat while accounting for twenty-two of the enemy. The theatre was a proving ground for the Sea Harrier in particular and the STOVL (Short Take-Off and Vertical Landing) concept in general, and it led directly to the much improved FA Mk 2, which soon after the conflict addressed the shortcomings (somewhat underarmed, ideally requiring a longer-range missile, lacking a 'look-down' capability in its radar system) and resolved them.

It must be said that, in addition to the skills of its pilots—both RN and RAF—the success of the aircraft owed a great deal to its weapons system, especially the AIM-9L Sidewinder missiles supplied at short notice by the United States. It was handicapped somewhat by its short range: the need to protect the two carriers from which the Sea Harriers were operating, *Invincible* and *Hermes*, dictated that they be based as far away as was reasonable from Argentine air bases, widening the radius of the CAPs (combat air patrols) that they had to fly and, in strike sorties, affording little loitering time over and around the target. Nevertheless, the deployment of the Sea Harriers was a resounding success—and the experiences of 1982 make it even more incomprehensible that the Royal Navy is being denied integrated air cover ('area defence') from 2006 inwards.

Sea Harriers have flown combat missions since the Falklands episode, for example during Operation 'Allied Force' in the Balkans in 1999, when seven FA.2s were deployed. One of these was lost to ground fire, the pilot being rescued by Special Air Service personnel.

Above: RAF Harrier GR.3s and RN Sea Harriers share *Hermes'* flight deck in a photograph taken during the Falklands War.

Left: Another photograph of *Hermes'* flight deck, this one taken just prior to the voyage to the Falklands. The aircraft would be repainted in more sombre colours en route to the South Atlantic.

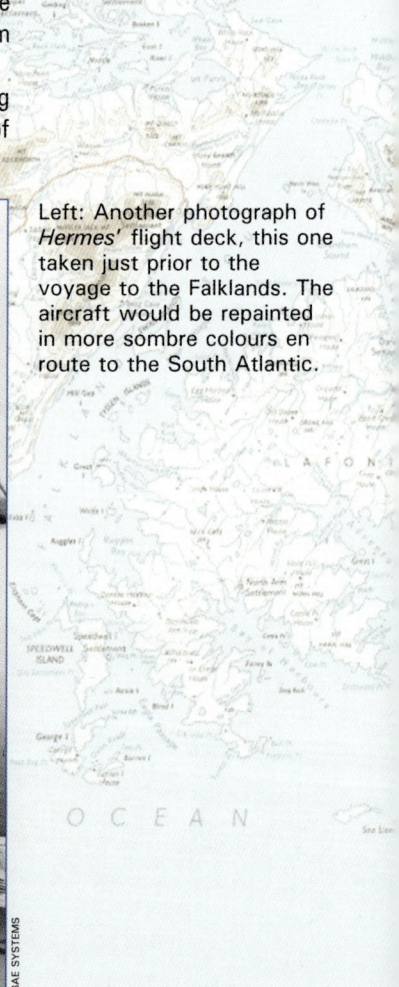

Above right: Two Sea Harriers returning from a sortie in the South Atlantic in May 1982 and about to perform the standard vertical landing aboard their carrier.

Right: A Sidewinder-armed Sea Harrier manoeuvres into position aboard a spray-clad flight deck, HMS *Hermes*,

FLEET AIR ARM SEA HARRIER COMBAT SUCCESSES, MAY–JUNE 1982

Date	Aircraft	Pilot	Victim	Method/remarks
1 May	XZ452	Flt Lt P. Barton RAF	Mirage IIIEA	Sidewinder
1 May	XZ455	Flt Lt Penfold RAF	Dagger A	Sidewinder
1 May	XZ451	Lt A. Curtis RN	Canberra B.62	Sidewinder
21 May	XZ457	Lt Morell RN	A-4Q Skyhawk	Cannon fire
21 May	XZ451	Lt-Cdr N. Ward RN	Pucara	Cannon fire
21 May	XZ496	Lt-Cdr Blissett RN	A-4C Skyhawk	Sidewinder
21 May	XZ492	Lt-Cdr Thomas RN	A-4C Skyhawk	Sidewinder
21 May	XZ455	Lt-Cdr Frederiksen RN	Dagger A	Sidewinder
21 May	ZA190	Lt Thomas RN	2 × Dagger A	Sidewinder; 2 victims in 1 sortie
21 May	ZA175	Lt-Cdr N. Ward RN	Dagger A	Sidewinder
21 May	XZ457	Lt Morell RN	A-4Q Skyhawk	Sidewinder
21 May	XZ500	Flt Lt Leeming RAF	A-4Q Skyhawk	Cannon fire
23 May	ZA194	Lt Hale RN	Dagger A	Sidewinder
23 May	ZA191	Flt-Lt Leeming RN	A.109A	Cannon fire; shared with ZA192
23 May	ZA192	Flt Lt D. Morgan RAF	A.109A	Cannon-fire; shared with ZA191
24 May	XZ457	Lt-Cdr A. Auld RN	2 × Dagger A	Sidewinder; 2 victims in 1 sortie
24 May	ZA193	Lt-Cdr Smith RN	Dagger A	Sidewinder
1 June	XZ451	Lt-Cdr N. Ward RN	C-130E Hercules	Sidewinder and cannon fire
8 June	ZA177	Flt Lt D. Morgan RAF	2 × A-4B Skyhawk	Sidewinder; 2 victims in 1 sortie
8 June	XZ499	Lt Smith RN	A-4B Skyhawk	Sidewinder

FIGHTER ATTACK

DESPITE the Sea Harrier's success in the South Atlantic during 1982, the aircraft was perceived to have shortcomings that would require rectification to enable it to perform adequately in the 1990s and beyond. Accordingly, it was announced, quite quickly after the cessation of hostilities, that a 'Phase I Update' would be put in hand immediately. This involved the facility to carry four instead of two short-range missiles (Sidewinders) and to carry enlarged (190-gallon) external fuel tanks, together with upgrades and improvements to ease the pilot's workload and assist with carrier-based take-offs and landings.

In 1985 came a further announcement that the aircraft would undergo a much more radical 'mid-life update': most existing Sea Harriers would be progressively upgraded, and a further eighteen brand new aircraft were contracted for in 1988. The changes were extensive internally though not that noticeable externally—other than the revised nose profile brought about by the installation of Blue Vixen pulse-Doppler radar, which now gave the aircraft a 'look-down-shoot-down' capability and required the characteristic nose pitot sensor to be relocated to the leading edge of the tailfin. The aircraft's potency was considerably enhanced by wiring it for the carriage of 'fire-and-forget' Advanced Medium-Range Anti-Aircraft Missiles (AMRAAM), up to four of which could be toted, one under each wing and two under the belly. The whole package gave the Sea Harrier the ability to 'track-while-scan' (i.e., look for other targets whilst tracking one in particular) and to destroy enemy aircraft 'beyond visual range', making it the most formidable fighter in any European air arm at that time. The cockpit was completely overhauled, with the installation of multi-function displays and a 'hands-on-throttle-and-stick' (HOTAS) system, while the nav/attack system and radar warning receiver (RWR) equipment was also enhanced. Dimensionally, a 14-inch 'plug' behind the wing trailing edge extended the fuselage so that new equipment could be accommodated; other, more cosmetic changes saw, for example, the deletion of the ram-air turbine atop the fuselage and some modification to the wing leading edges.

NEW DESIGNATION

The multi-role capability of the FRS.1 was retained—the aircraft could carry bombs, rockets and so forth for ground attack sorties if required—although ironically the anti-shipping role, for which the aircraft at long last received qualification in the mid-1980s in conjunction with the BAe Sea Eagle, was withdrawn from use just as the upgraded aircraft had joined the squadrons. Carrier qualification trials were carried out aboard *Ark Royal* late in 1990, and the first

Below: Two FA.2s flank an FRS.1 on board *Invincible* in the Adriatic during the Balkans Emergency, late June 1994. No squadron markings are evident on the aircraft fully in the frame.
Right, top: Most Sea Harrier FA.2s were conversions of existing FRS.1s; ZE692, for example, first flew as an FRS.1 in December 1987 but was upgraded a few years later and returned to the Navy in August 1995.
Right, centre: No squadron markings are evident on this aircraft either, although it is assigned to 899 NAS at Yeovilton and is here being readied for flight, 2004. However, the fin bears traces of the 800 NAS emblem: there was a great deal of 'chopping and changing' of unit markings amongst Sea Harriers as the limited number of aircraft on strength were moved around the squadrons.
Right, bottom: ZH806/'122' stowed below aboard *Ark Royal*, February 2004. 'If it doesn't move, paint it; if it does, salute it . . . or, on board an aircraft carrier, lash it down!' CBLS (Carrier, Bomb, Light Store) components are evident in the hangar screen racks.

RICHARD L. WARD

RICHARD L. WARD

AD HOC PUBLICATIONS

HOWARD CARROLL

Left: ZD582 at Yeovilton in 1996, equipped with cannon pods, long-range tanks and a CBLS (Carrier, Bomb, Light Store) under the belly. Unusually for an unattended static aircraft, the intakes are unprotected by FOD (Foreign Object Damage) guards.
Right: FA.2 ZE690 displaying the bolt-on in-flight refuelling probe sometimes by the Sea Harrier carried for extended flights.

aircraft was handed over to the Navy in April 1993. The first of the brand new (as opposed to converted) Sea Harriers was delivered in October 1995 and the last in 1999.

Along with the redelivered aircraft came a changing designation. The replacement was at first referred to as the Sea Harrier Fighter Reconnaissance Strike Mark Two (FRS Mk 2), but this was quickly changed to Fighter/Attack Mark Two (F/A Mk 2); and eventually the solidus was dropped. Technically, the original Sea Harrier had a reconnaissance capability, although as the recce pod reportedly devised for the aircraft had never actually seen service with it the 'R' in the designation could only be justified by the retention of the sideways-looking F.35 wet-film camera in the starboard side of the nose—which was, in truth, not much of a justification at all. 'A' rather than 'S' presumably reflected the abandonment of the nuclear role, which the original Sea Harrier certainly had, in favour of conventional attack warfare.

Below: Final days: two of the last Sea Harrier FA.2s remaining at RNAS Yeovilton. The withdrawal of the type from service leaves the Royal Navy without indigenous area defence cover for the next six (or more) years.

WITHDRAWAL

When the FA.2 was in delivery, it was anticipated that the aircraft would remain in service for two decades of so, pending the arrival of two new fleet carriers and their fixed-wing air group, made up of the Lockheed-Martin F-35C Joint Strike Fighter (JSF). However, in 2002 it became known that the aircraft would be withdrawn as early as 2006; reportedly, the Pegasus 106 was beginning to give serious trouble as a result of a programme to strengthen its fan blades, causing unacceptable vibration and requiring too-frequent (and too costly) replacement. As these words are written (March 2006), the last remaining Sea Harriers are indeed leaving FAA service, but the whole question of FAA fixed-wing re-equipment is in a state of some confusion. The plan for the Short Take-Off/Vertical Landing (STOVL) version of the JSF, the F-35C, to equip Royal Navy squadrons from 2012 is officially in place, but the question of the Sea Harrier's 'replacement' is nevertheless one of fluidity. In the meantime, and until the conundrum is resolved, FAA air crews continue to fly Harriers, albeit as part of the Joint Force Harrier (JFH) (sic) and only in the ground-attack/tactical strike role with Harrier GR.7s and 9s.

NAVY T-BIRDS

THOUGH decidedly not *Sea* Harriers, a small number of two-seat aircraft were supplied for use both by the Royal Navy and the Indian Navy for the purposes of training air crews, and it is appropriate to accord them very brief reference here. The Fleet Air Arm, having originally utilised one or two RAF-operated T Mk 2s, took delivery of four T Mk 4Ns following the 1982 Falklands War and these were allocated to the Headquarters Squadron, 899 NAS. The latter aircraft were fitted with the uprated Pegasus Mk 104 and basic Sea Harrier avionics. To complement the FA.2 when it entered service, a small number of two-seat T.8s were taken on strength, upgraded internally better to simulate the new Sea Harrier's facilities.

Right: One of the first BAe Sea Harrier T.4N trainers. The aircraft have a combat capability though of course this is handicapped by their lack of radar.

Left: A pair of T Mk 8s at Yeovilton in 2004, resplendent in their immaculate glossy black finish.
Right, lower: An Indian Navy Harrier trainer, designated T Mk 60 by the aircraft's manufacturers. Like the Sea Harriers, these are assigned to No 300 ('White Tigers') Squadron.
Below: One of the pair of former RAF Harrier trainers, overhauled and supplied to the Indian Navy as attrition replacements. Somewhat incongruously, the characteristic 'Snoopy' nose—for the RAF's laser rangefinder—is retained on these aircraft

AD HOC PUBLICATIONS

ROYAL NAVY

SIMON WATSON

SIMON WATSON

SQUADRONS & COLOURS

WITH the disbandment of the fleet carrier fixed-wing squadrons—892 with Phantoms and 809 with Buccaneers—in mid-December 1978 following the withdrawal from service of HMS *Ark Royal*, there was a six-month hiatus before the Fleet Air Arm was once more flying fixed-wing combat aircraft. However, it would be a further twelve months before the FAA could once more deploy to sea in earnest: the first of the new light aircraft carriers, HMS *Invincible*, would not commission until the summer of 1980.

The Navy of course put the intervening period to good use, training pilots, technicians and maintenance personnel, honing the servicing, electronics and weapons systems and ironing out the few 'wrinkles' evident in the aircraft—in short, 'working up'. Carrier compatibility trials were conducted and flight-deck procedures perfected on board HMS *Hermes*, the former light fleet (and later commando) carrier, which would, it transpired, fly the Sea Harrier operationally owing to delays in the completion of the *Invincible* class ships.

The first Sea Harrier for the Navy was delivered from the British Aerospace flight-test centre at Dunsfold, Surrey, to RNAS Yeovilton, Somerset, on 18 June 1979, there to be joined over the ensuing weeks by a further half-dozen aircraft to form 700A Flight, the so-called intensive Flying Trials Unit. This unit was redesignated 899 Naval Air Squadron in March the following year, in keeping with the practice established in the early 1960s of bestowing this 'numberplate' on the FAA's Headquarters Squadron. At the same time, the first of what were intended to be two front-line Sea Harrier squadrons was commissioned at Yeovilton when 800 NAS, previously equipped with Buccaneers in the late 1960s and early 1970s, was re-formed with, nominally, six aircraft; it was joined in January 1981 by 801 NAS, with a similar establishment.

Until the outbreak of hostilities between Great Britain and Argentina in April 1982, RN Sea Harriers were finished in the familiar and very smart scheme of Dark Sea Grey uppersurfaces

Below: XZ451, one of the first Sea Harriers to be delivered to the Fleet Air Arm, showing the distinctive fin *décor* of 700A Flight. This particular aircraft went on to achieve 'kills' over the Falklands in the hands of Lieutenant Curtis RN and Lieutenant-Commander Ward RN. It subsequently crashed off Sardinia during a training exercise in 1989, the pilot ejecting safely.

FLEET AIR ARM SEA HARRIER SQUADRONS

Unit	Base	Mark(s)	Dates	Remarks
700A Flight	Yeovilton	FRS.1	18 Jun 1979–31 Mar 1980	Intensive Flying Trials Unit (IFTU).
899 NAS	Yeovilton	FRS.1, FA.2	31 Mar 1980–31 Mar 2005	Evolved from IFTU. Training squadron.
800 NAS	Yeovilton	FRS.1, FA.2	31 Mar 1980–31 Mar 2004	First front-line Sea Harrier unit.
801 NAS	Yeovilton	FRS.1, FA.2	Jan 1981–31 Mar 2006	
809 NAS	Yeovilton	FRS.1	6 Apr–17 Dec 1982	Formed as a result of Operation 'Corporate'.

RICHARD L. WARD

Above: 800 Naval Air Squadron line-up. This unit was the first of the three front-line sea Harrier units to form, in March 1980. The 'N' code on the fin tip denotes HMS *Invincible*.

Below: XZ493, while serving with 801 NAS. This aircraft is currently displayed in the Fleet Air Arm Museum at Yeovilton, wearing this same paint scheme.

and white undersurfaces, the paintwork having a distinct semi-gloss character. The roundels, in the six standard positions, were Type 'D' and the 'Royal Navy' legend, base code and aircraft call-sign appeared in white; the serial numbers, bold underwing and minuscule on the ventral tail fillet, were in black. Squadron insignia were emblazoned across the width of the tail fin. The outbreak of hostilities in 1982 was to change everything.

As the Royal Navy Task Force proceeded south towards the Falkland Islands in April 1982, the embarked Sea Harriers underwent a radical change in their appearance, in keeping with the requirement to render them less easily visible during flying operations. Central to the objective was to remove all traces of white paint, so that no sharp contrasts could be offered to watching eyes. Thus, *in general terms*, both 800 and 801 NAS aircraft were given a coat of Extra Dark Sea Grey, the white-painted components of the national markings were overpainted, and lettering and unit insignia were either overpainted in black or removed altogether. It should be emphasised that the measures taken were a good deal more involved than this, and that, owing to the exigencies of the situation, there was a great deal of variation in the finished appearance of the aircraft so treated; it is not possible to give more detailed information in the limited space available in this book, and, furthermore, there was a good deal of aircraft interchange amongst the three principal units.

BAE SYSTEMS

RICHARD L. WARD

Left, upper: The winged fist of 899 NAS displayed on a Sea Harrier in the early Dark Sea Grey/white scheme.
Left, lower: The Medium Sea Grey/'Barley Grey' scheme adopted for the short-lived commission of 809 Naval Air Squadron gave this unit's Sea Harriers a very pale appearance. This is ZA193.
Right: Detail views of 809's markings.
Below: ZA177/'77' on board *Hermes* following the carrier's return from the Falklands deployment, July 1982. No fin markings are present, although in fact the aircraft is assigned to 800 NAS.
Background image: 809 NAS line-up at Yeovilton prior to the unit's departure to the South Atlantic, 1982.

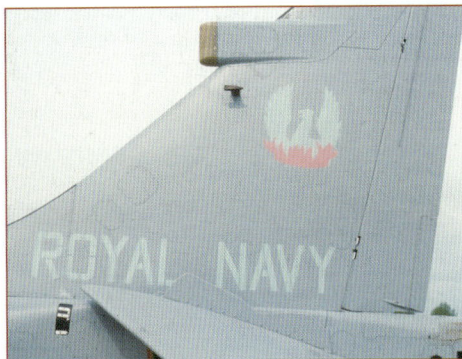

The emergency re-formation of 809 Naval Air Squadron in April 1982—with, for the most part, aircraft hitherto assigned to 899 NAS—also resulted in a change of colour scheme, but in this instance two shades of medium grey were employed. These Sea Harriers were finished in Medium Sea Grey except for the undersurfaces of the wings and tailplane, which were painted Grey BS4800.18.B.21 (the so-called 'Barley Grey'); all exterior markings appeared in pink or pale blue as appropriate. Meanwhile the remaining aircraft in the Sea Harrier establishment were also 'toned down' in appearance.

In the months following the conclusion of hostilities on 14 June, and with the experience of the conflict to the forefront, a new, more or less standard scheme was adopted for Sea Harriers,

Above: 809 Naval Air Squadron on sortie, *en masse.*

and following their next major servicing the aircraft emerged with an overall coat of Dark Sea Grey.

MARK TWO SERVICE

Deliveries of the upgraded version of the Sea Harrier, the FA Mk 2, got under way on 2 April 1993 and the new mark gradually supplanted the FRS.1 over the following months; by the end of 1995 all three Sea Harrier units—Nos 800, 801 and 899 Naval Air Squadrons—had completely re-equipped with replacement aircraft and the FRS.1 had disappeared from the Royal Navy's inventory.

Left: The return to peacetime conditions saw Sea Harriers retain their sombre grey finish overall, but squadron markings were reintroduced and regularised. This pair of aircraft display the new-style 801 NAS winged trident and chequerboard.

Left: Toned-down: an 899 NAS Sea Harrier FRS.1 seen shortly after the Falklands War.

British Aerospace Sea Harrier FRS Mk 1
801 Naval Air Squadron, February 1981

100

001

N

ROYAL NAVY

XZ493

001

ROYAL NAVY

001

XZ493

XZ493

XZ493

RC06

British Aerospace Sea Harrier FA Mk 2
800 Naval Air Squadron, March 2004

ROYAL NAVY

ZD613

122

800 N
1980 - 2

800
1980

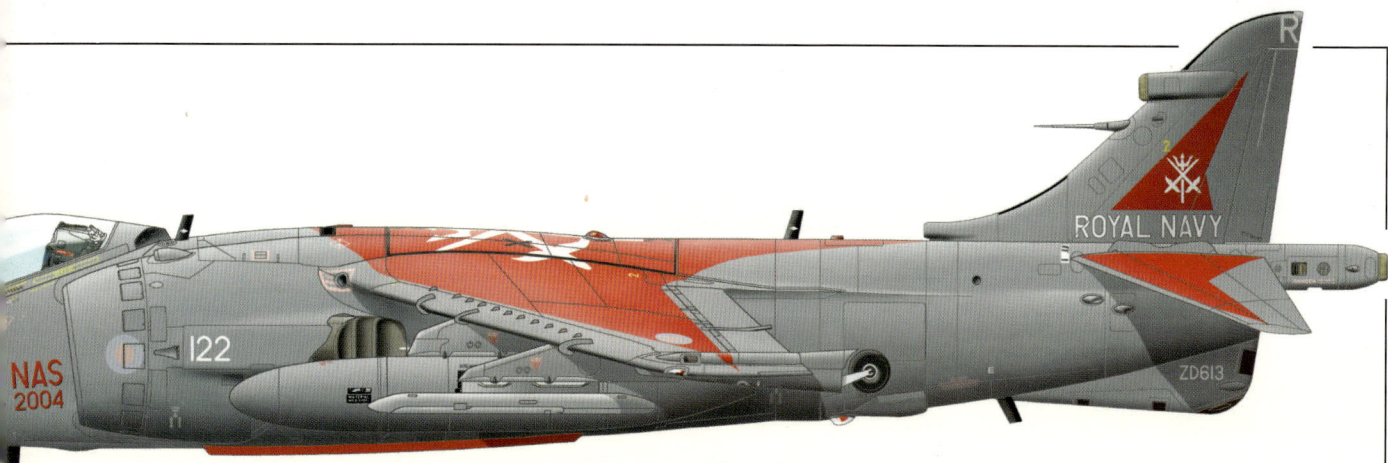

ROYAL NAVY

NAS
2004

122

ZD613

R

RC06

Above and below: An 899 NAS Sea Harrier FA Mk 2, at Yeovilton in 2004.

The story of the FA.2's colour schemes is less fraught than that of its predecessor. There have been variations (as a study of the photographs in this book will show), but, in general, by the time the aircraft entered service the finish had settled down as Medium Sea Grey (BS381C:637) overall. As always, however, the effects of weathering—particularly after long periods spent at sea—had an influence, and some diversity in both hue and intensity of colour could always be noted. The radomes, in particular, were susceptible to variation, while 899

KRISTOF JONCKHEERE

RICHARD L. WARD

Left: The 2004 display Sea Harrier from 899 NAS, in Roundel Blue and white. Above: FA.2 fin markings: 899 (left) and 800 NAS. Below: Aircraft of 899 NAS in 1996.

NAS's 'winged fist' insignia saw a number of different interpretations. The carriers to which the two front-line squadrons were assigned at any time were indicated on the aircraft tailfin tips by the individual code letters 'N' (*Invincible*), 'L' (*Illustrious*) or 'R' (*Ark Royal*), 899 generally displaying the 'VL' code signifying RNAS Yeovilton. 'Special' schemes on Sea Harriers of both marks were something of a rarity, but 800 NAS did sign off in 2004 with a rampant display of colour (see pages 31–32).

IN DETAIL

This spread: The installation of the new Blue Vixen radar suite in the Sea Harrier FA.2 required the remodelling of the radome, giving the nose of the aircraft a rather less elegant, semi-bulbous profile; it also required the relocation of the nose-mounted pitot tube, and this was shifted to a position along the leading edge of the tailfin. The FA.2 also had additional intakes and sensors on the lower contours of the nose, and the ventral Doppler panel on the FRS.1 (bottom left) was deleted; both variants had the F95 ('wet film') camera port on the starboard side. The reaction control valve (RCV) installed beneath the nose—one of four such installations on the aircraft, enabling the pilot to make attitude adjustments when the aircraft is hovering or flying below stalling speed—can be seen with its tell-tale exhaust streak. The photograph opposite top was taken on board *Illustrious* at Malta in November 2005.

AD HOC PUBLICATIONS

AD HOC PUBLICATIONS

AD HOC PUBLICATIONS

CHARLES POLIDANO

RICHARD L. WARD

AD HOC PUBLICATIONS

AD HOC PUBLICATIONS

AD HOC PUBLICATIONS

Above left: Port intake detail, FRS.1. The non-standard roundel has been produced by the simple expedient of overpainting the white of the original Type 'D'. The early style of intake FOD guard can be glimpsed at left. Below: General view over the starboard wing of the FRS.1. Right, upper: Port intake detail, FA.2, showing the more efficient inflatable FOD guard adopted later.

Right, lower: The bolt-on in-flight refuelling probe, here installed on an FA.2; the same piece of equipment was available to the FRS Mk 1. All these views show the typical attitude of the auxiliary intake doors for an inactive aircraft; they were non-mechanical, and therefore subject to gravity.

MATERIAL
MILD STEEL

EXPLOSIVE
RELEASE

AD HOC PUBLICATIONS

DANGER
AIRCRAFT
ON JACKS

AD HOC PUBLICATIONS

This spread: The forward and after nozzles were of a different design, and although on the FRS.1 the forward ('cold') nozzles were generally painted the same colour as the airframe, those on the FA.2 appear to have had a universally brownish hue. The after nozzles had deflector plates to keep the hot exhaust gases away from the airframe proper. The deflection angle could be checked externally by means of a scale marked off in 10-degree increments; slight rotation forward was possible, giving the aircraft a measure of reverse thrust—as seen at every air display, but also providing a useful manoeuvring capability both in the air and on the flight deck. The photograph at bottom left shows an FA.2 with its Pegasus removed for maintenance; it may be noted that it was not necessary to remove the forward nozzles in order to change an engine. The aerodynamically faired 'blade' (immediately below) is a fuel vent.

SIMON WATSON

Left: A mechanic carries out some checks on an Indian Navy Sea Harrier. The row of vortex generators and the two stub wing fences are clearly shown, as is the starboard wing-tip RCV outlet. In contrast to Royal Navy practice, stencilling, warning notices and panels and component identification codes are here dark grey rather than red or pale red. This page: FRS.1 and FA.2 wing detail compared: the deletion of the inboard 'dog-tooth' and of one of the vortex generators, and the added leading-edge stub fence, on the later mark are all clearly visible. The dual-purpose aperture at the wing-root leading edge served both as a cooling intake for the Pegasus engine and as an entry point for a fire hose in the event of an engine fire.

This spread: Sea Harrier tails. The characteristic tail boom housed the rear RCV, with the radar warning receiver fairing at its tip (the complementary forward-looking RWR being mounted on the leading edge of the tailfin). The exhaust outlets beneath the tailplane's leading edge on the FA.2 differed from the arrangement on the FRS.1 (seen bottom left). The background image features RNAS Yeovilton's 'ski-jump' facility. During the aircraft's final weeks in service the 801 NAS tail emblem (main photograph, right) sported the somewhat melancholy omega symbol to mark the passing of the aircraft.

ROYAL NAVY

ZH796

ZH810

ZH797

NEIL JONES

AD HOC PUBLICATIONS

This spread: Aspects of the Sea Harrier's bicycle/outrigger landing gear, identical for both marks—and almost so to that of the early RAF Harrier apart from having lash-down lugs for secure stowage aboard ship. The interior of the speed brake—the latter located immediately aft of the twin mainwheels—is shown opposite centre right. The recording of the names of servicing crews along the nosewheel doors was characteristic of FA.2s rather more than of FRS.1s.

AD HOC PUBLICATIONS

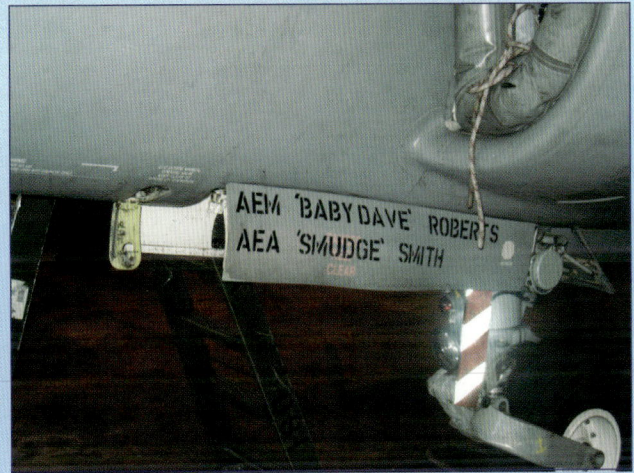

AEM 'BABY DAVE' ROBERTS
AEA 'SMUDGE' SMITH

WEAPONRY

AD HOC PUBLICATIONS

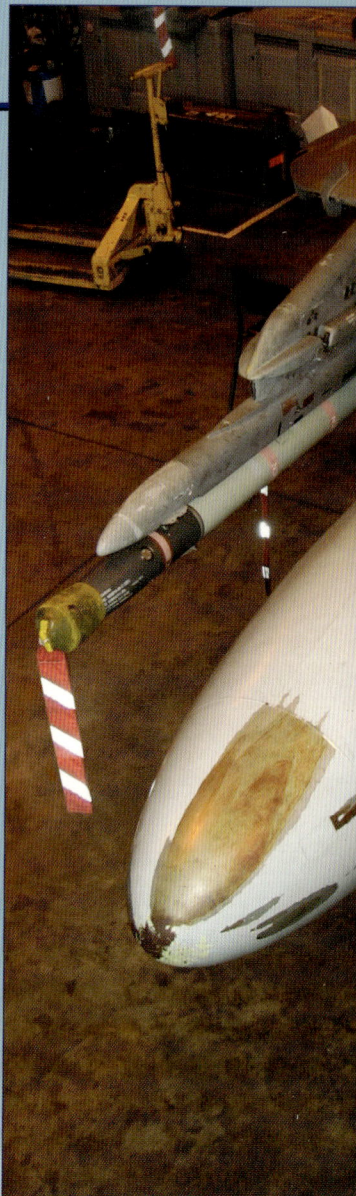

AD HOC PUBLICATIONS

AD HOC PUBLICATIONS

AD HOC PUBLICATIONS

ROYAL ORDNANCE

Above left: Two photographs showing details of the AIM-9L Sidewinder fit, FRS Mk 1. The inboard wing stations are here carrying the original 100-gallon long-range fuel tanks.

Left: The Sea Harrier's two detachable, underbelly 30mm Aden gun pods; the same weapon was fitted for both marks of the aircraft in Royal Navy service. The lower photograph shows the cannon in its unpodded state.

Above centre:: The Falklands War confirmed the view that the Sea Harrier required greater range, and the 190-gallon wing tank was introduced as a result, as shown on this FA.2. An acquisition Sidewinder round is carried outboard.

Top right: An FRS.2 configured to test-fly the BAe Sea Eagle anti-ship missile. During the Falklands conflict, the Argentinians recovered the remains of a Sea Harrier wired to carry this weapon even though the missile itself had not been issued to the RN—and reportedly modified their naval tactics as a result.

Above right: Indian Sea Harriers are configured to carry the Matra R.550 Magic anti-aircraft missile rather than the Sidewinder, as shown in this mock-up.

Below: The FA.2, uniquely, was equipped to carry the US AIM-120 Advanced Medium-Range Anti-Aircraft Missile (AMRAAM). A maximum of four could be toted, as shown on this test aircraft.

INSIDE INFO

RICHARD L. WARD

Left: The rearward-sliding hood, with Miniature Detonating Cord (MDC) evident. The scalloped rear contours of the canopy framework assure clearance of the twin dorsal antennas when the hood is opened.

Below left: Cockpit layout, FRS Mk 1. The unique feature— the nozzle control lever— is seen in the throttle box at left. When positioned fully forward (as here) the nozzles point directly aft.

Below right: Detail behind the pilot's ejection seat, FA Mk 2.

Bottom: Two views of the Martin-Baker Type 10H ejection seat which equips Sea Harriers. This example lacks the headpad fitted as standard.

Right: The upgraded cockpit of the FA Mk 2 (seat removed here). The primary changes were the addition of MFDs (multi-function displays), HOTAS (hands-on-throttle-and-stick) control technology stick and up-front control panel.

BAE SYSTEMS

AD HOC PUBLICATIONS

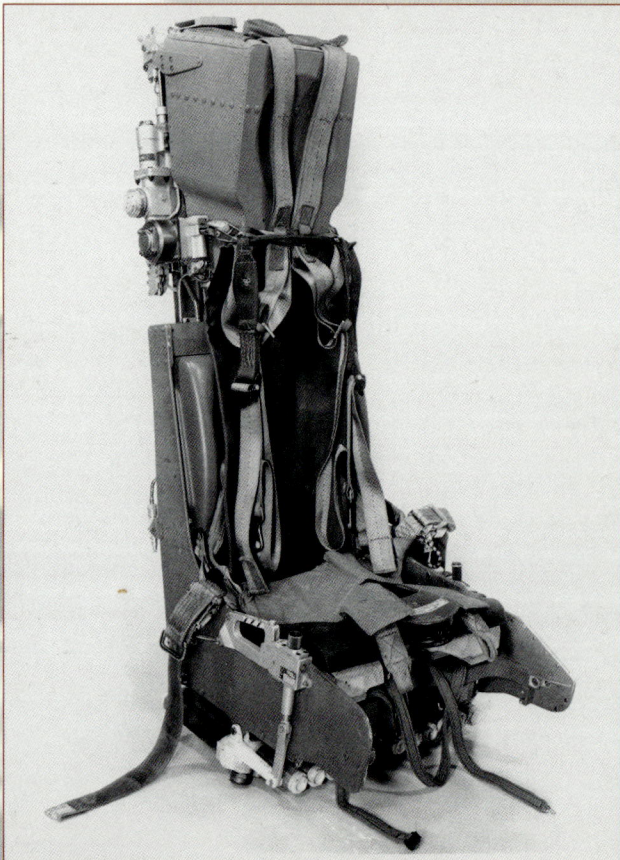

MARTIN-BAKER AIRCRAFT CO.

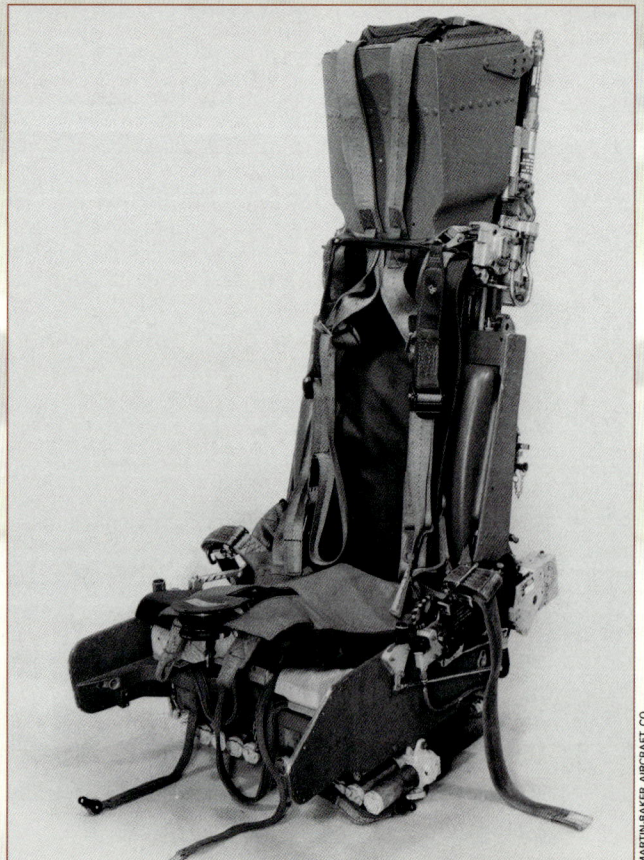

MARTIN-BAKER AIRCRAFT CO.

AD HOC PUBLICATIONS

SCALE PLANS

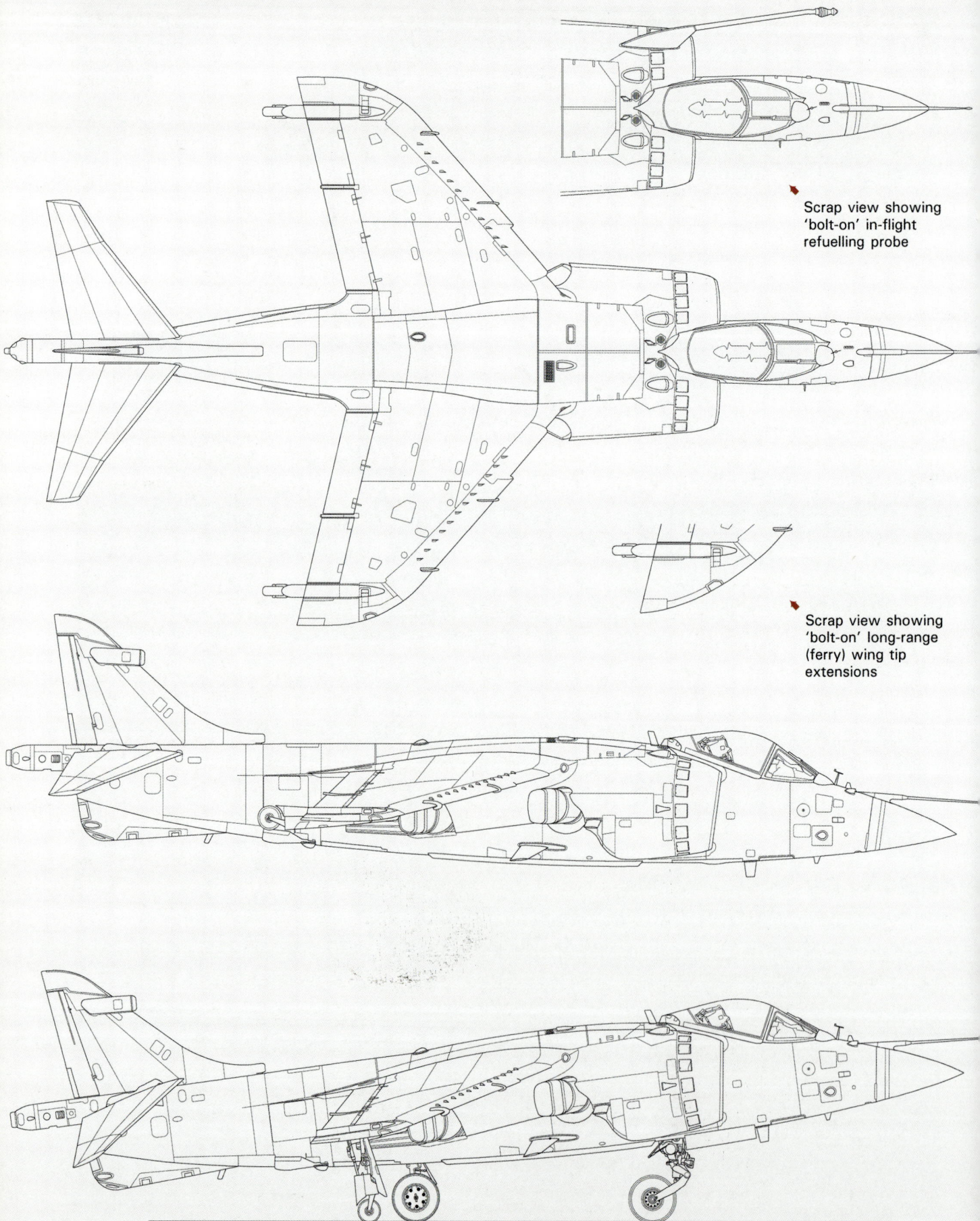

Scrap view showing 'bolt-on' in-flight refuelling probe

Scrap view showing 'bolt-on' long-range (ferry) wing tip extensions

BRITISH AEROSPACE SEA HARRIER FRS Mk 1

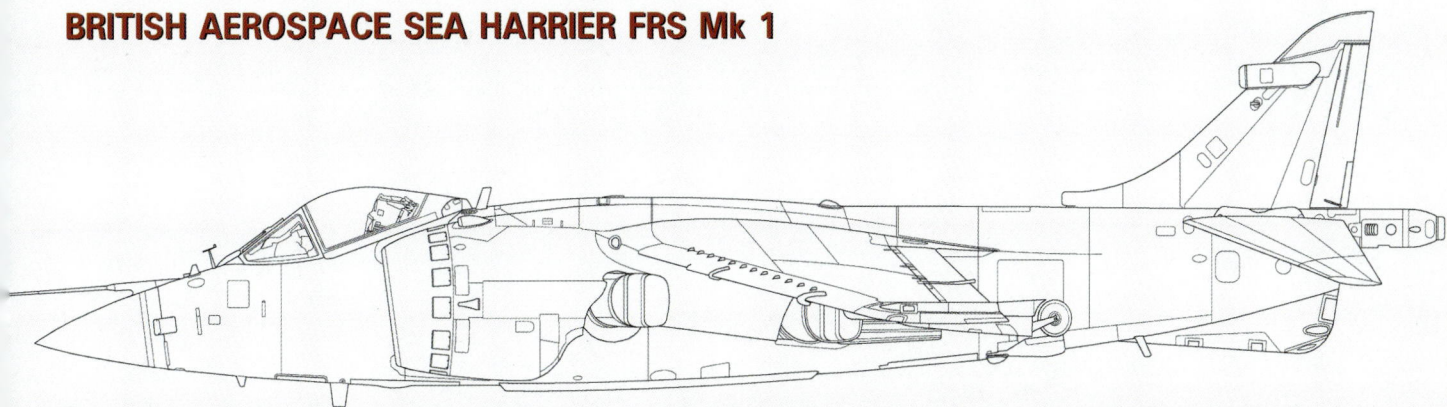

Scrap view showing
pylon fairings (fitted
when pylons
removed)

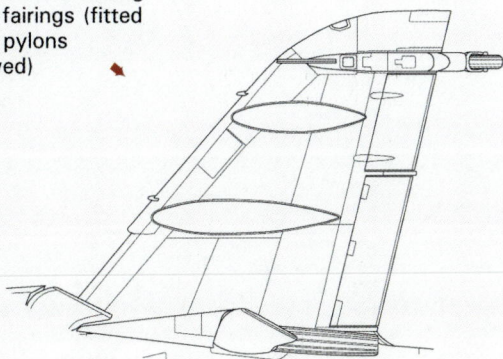

Scrap profile
view showing
30mm Aden
cannon units

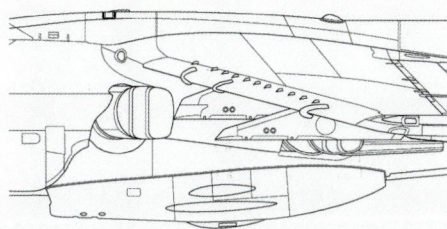

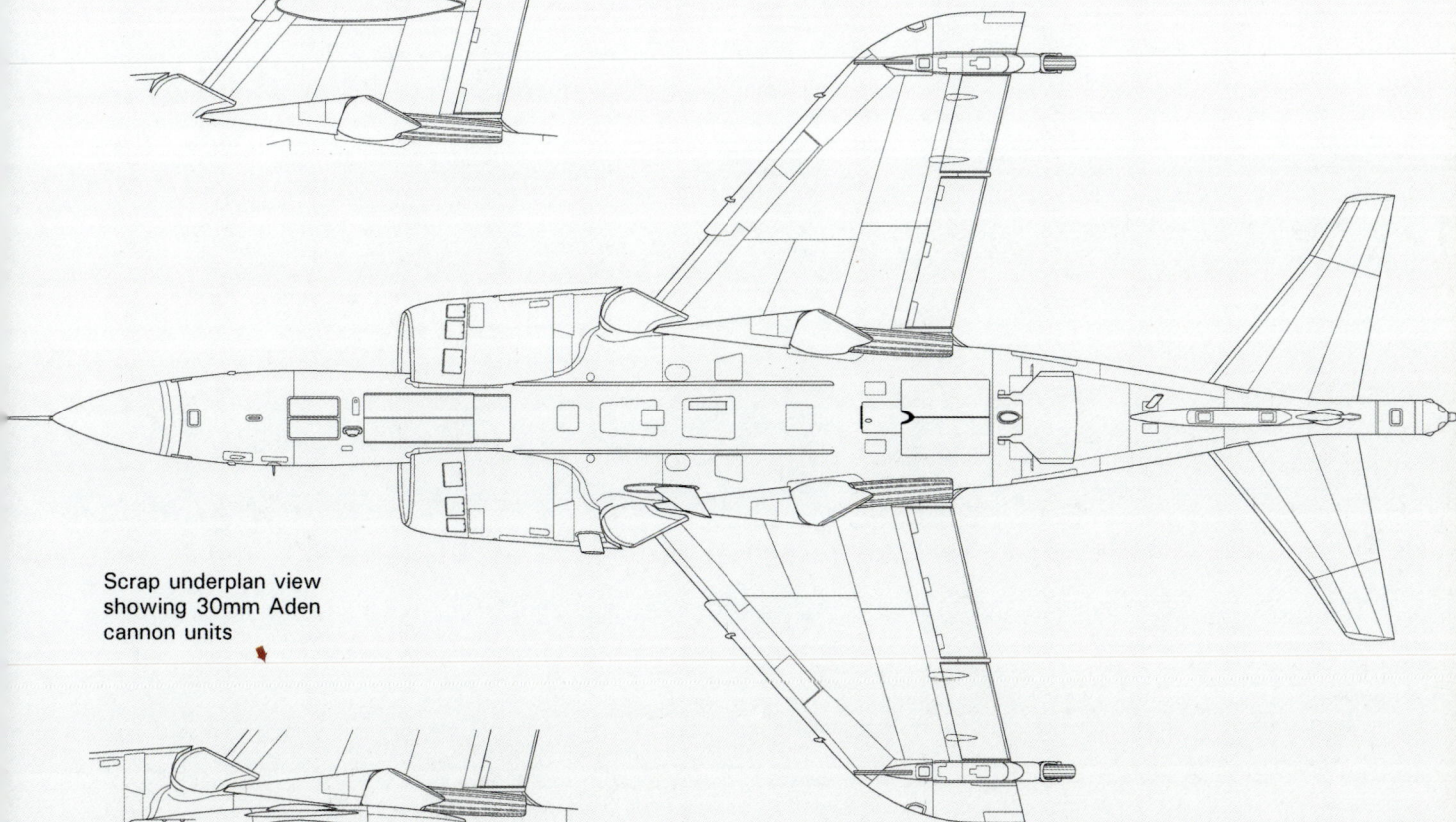

Scrap underplan view
showing 30mm Aden
cannon units

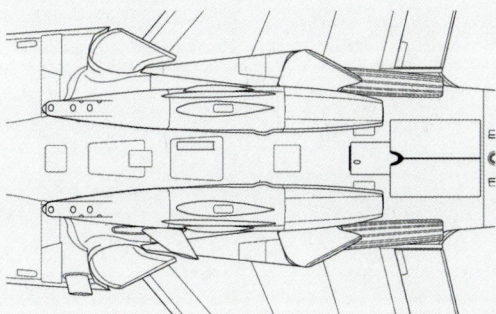

0   5   10 feet

1/72 scale

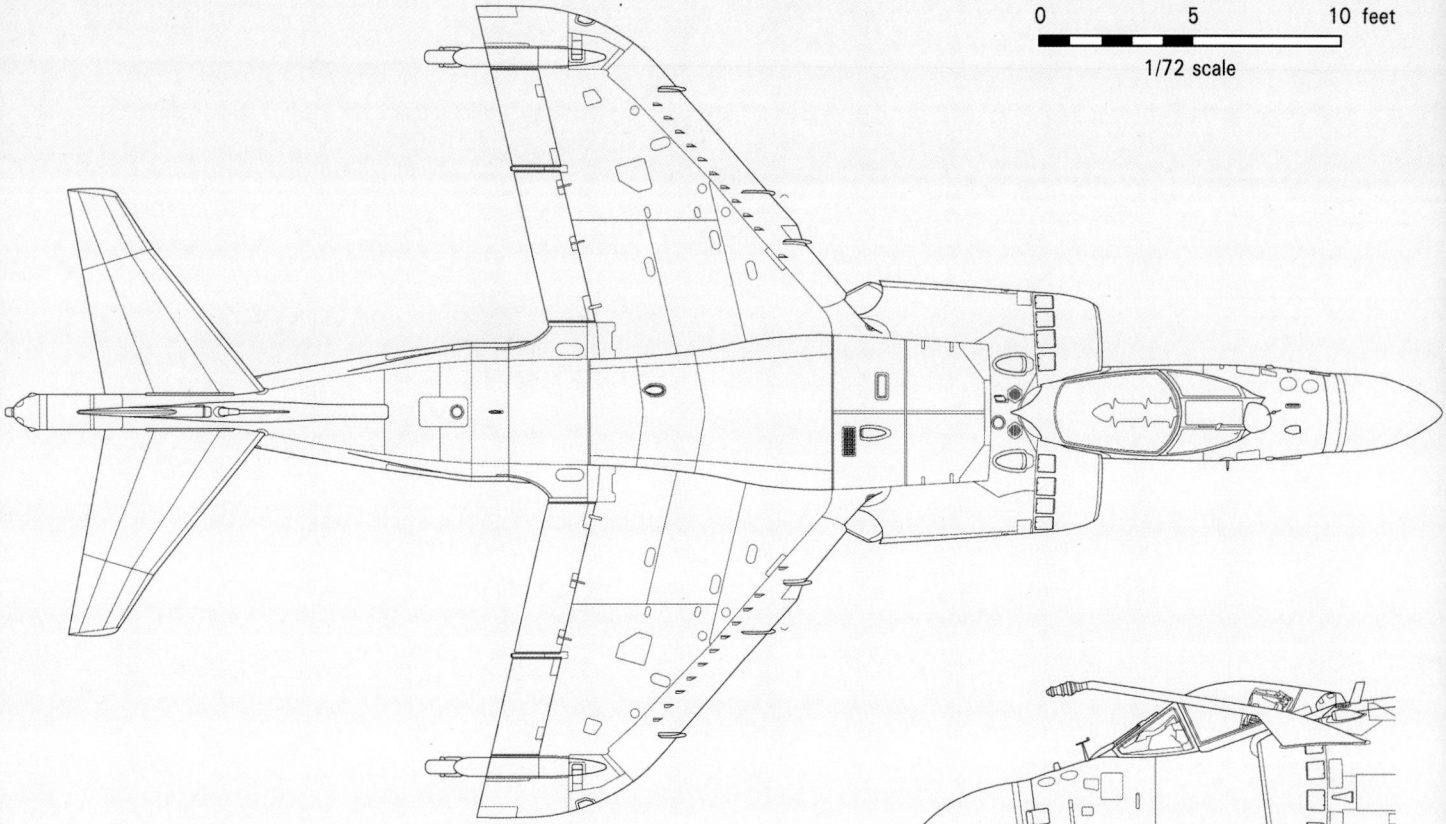

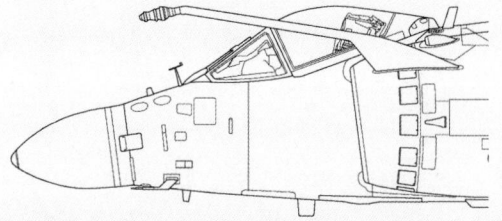

Scrap view showing 'bolt-on'
in-flight refuelling probe

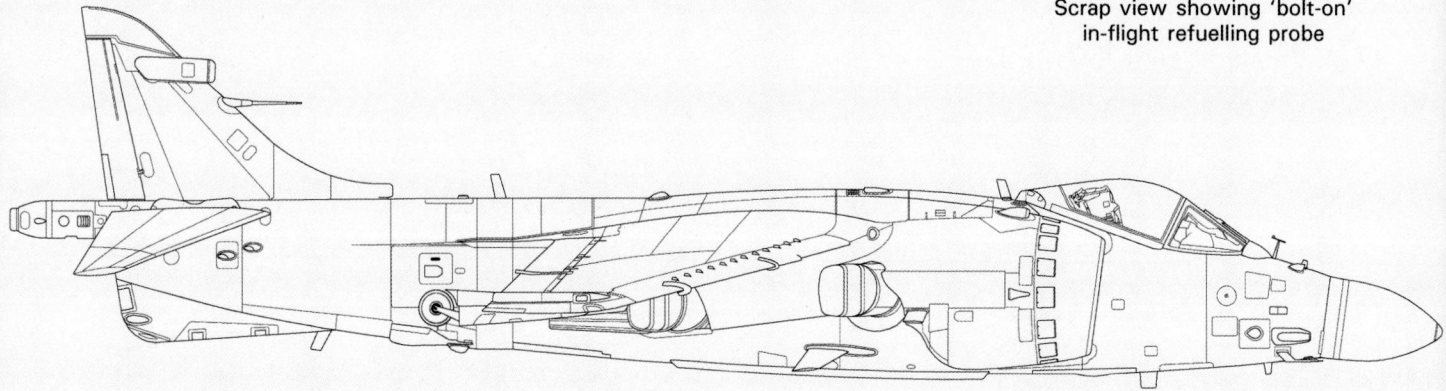

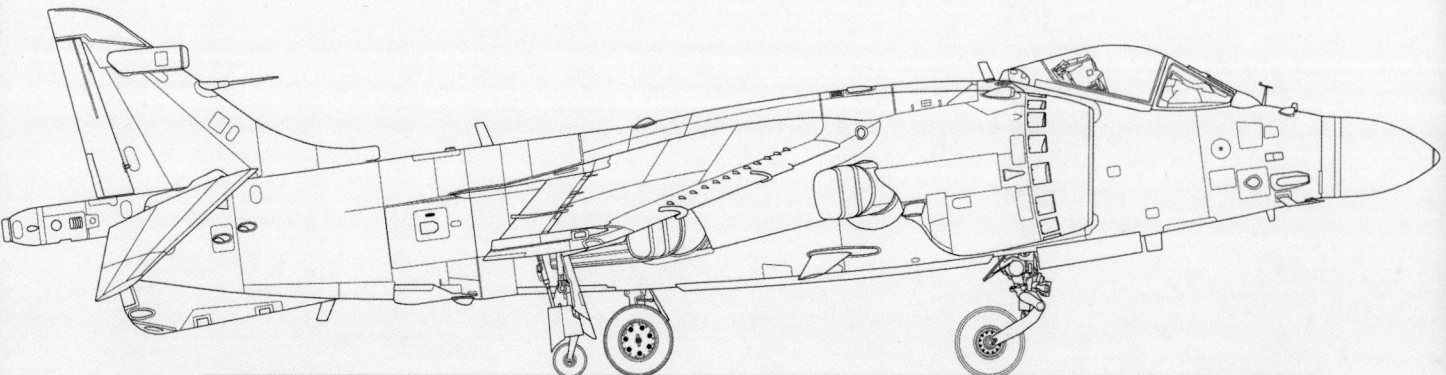

54 SEA HARRIER

0   5   10 feet

1/72 scale

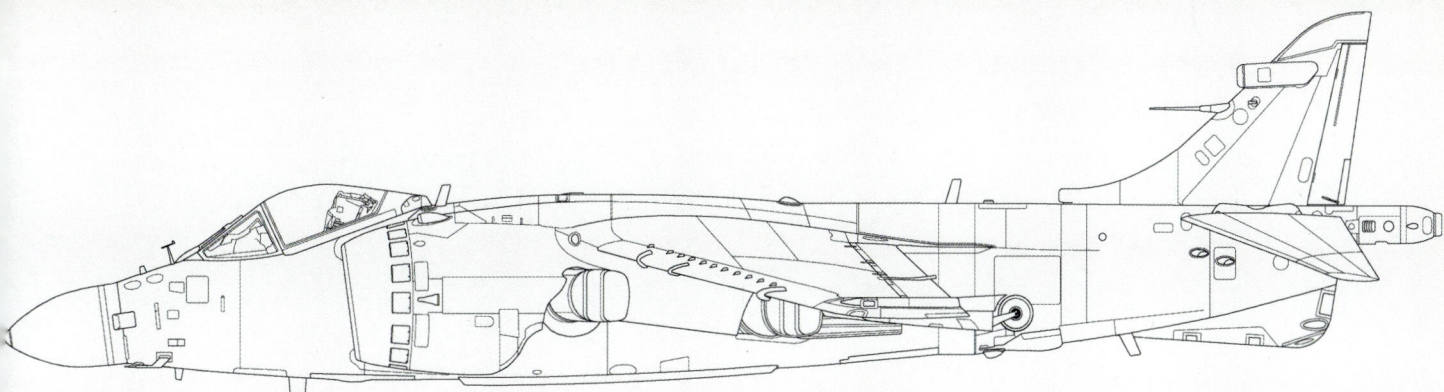

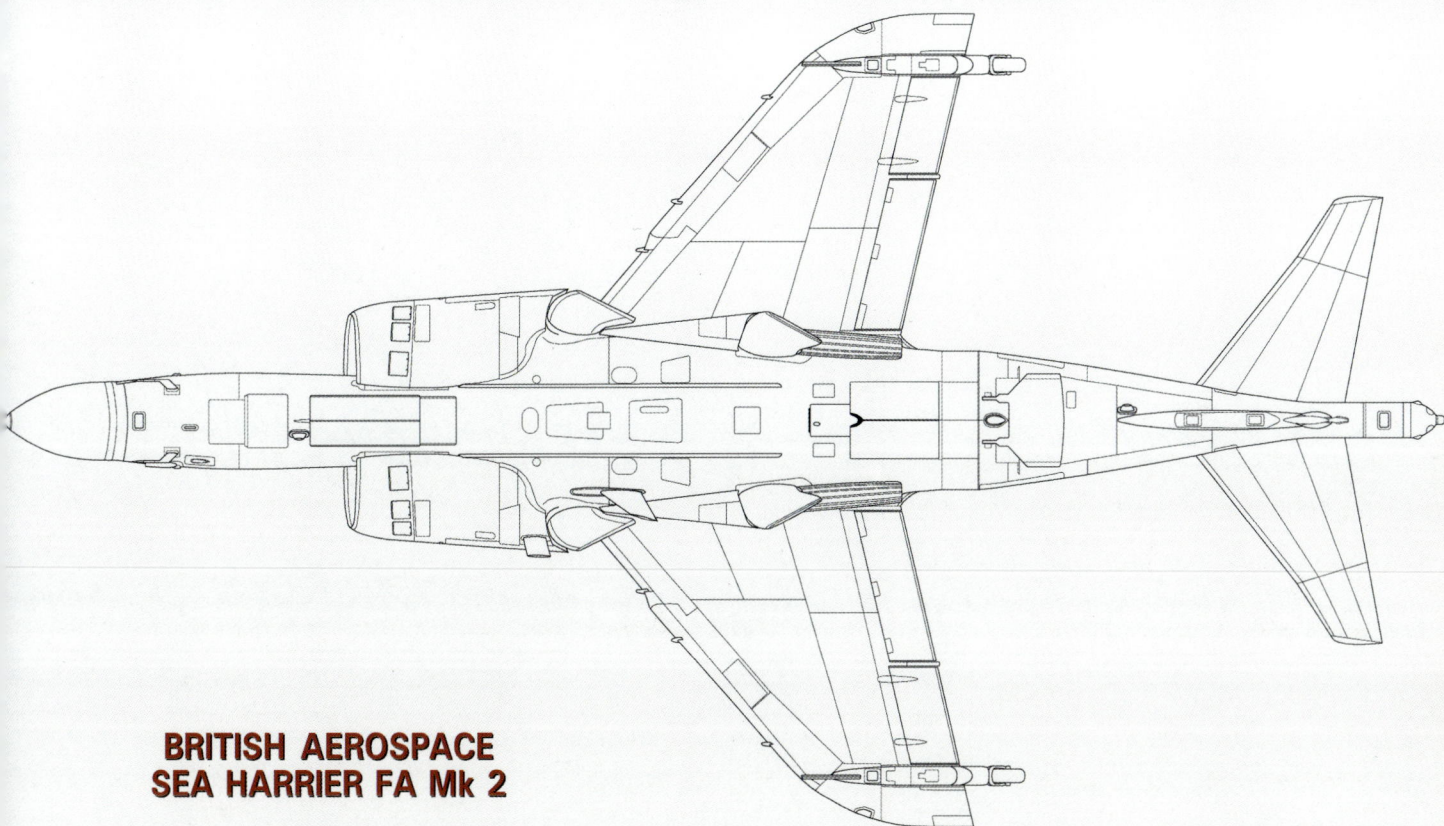

BRITISH AEROSPACE
SEA HARRIER FA Mk 2

BRITISH AEROSPACE SEA HARRIER SPECIFICATIONS

	FRS Mk 1	FA Mk 2
Engine	One Rolls-Royce Pegasus Mk 104 rated at 21,500lb	One Rolls-Royce Pegasus Mk 106 rated at 21,500lb
Dimensions		
Length	47ft 6½in	46ft 6in
Wingspan	25ft 3in	As FRS Mk 1
Height	12ft 2in	As FRS Mk 1
Wing area	201.1 sq ft	As FRS Mk 1
Empty weight	13,100lb	13,250lb
Take-off weight (max.)	26,200lb	26,250lb
Performance		
Max. speed	740mph (640kts, M 0.97) at sea level	730mph (635kts, M 0.96) at sea level
Tactical radius	465 miles	As FRS Mk 1
Range (combat)	620 miles	As FRS Mk 1
Range (ferry)	2,050 miles	As FRS Mk 1
Ceiling (max.)	51,000ft	As FRS Mk 1
Rate of climb	50,000ft/min.	As FRS Mk 1
Warload (max.)	2 × 30mm Aden cannon (optional) plus 5,000lb on pylons	As FRS Mk 1

BRITISH AEROSPACE SEA HARRIER
WEAPONS AND STORES

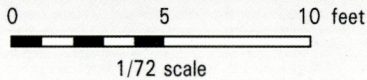

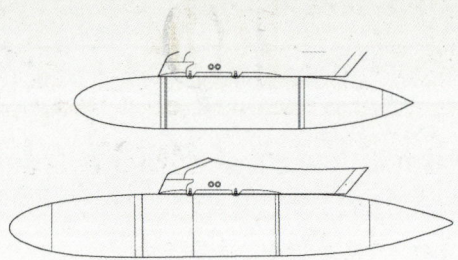

0   5   10 feet
1/72 scale

External fuel tank (inboard pylon):
100-gallon (upper) and 190-gallon

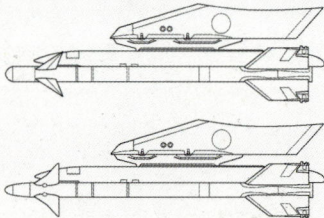

Sidewinder: AIM-9G (upper;
FRS Mk 1 only) and AIM-9L on outboard pylon

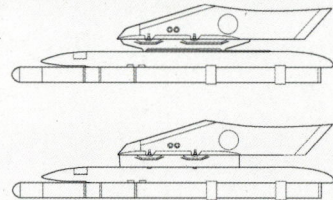

Sidewinder acquisition round (outboard pylon),
showing adaptor rails of differing design

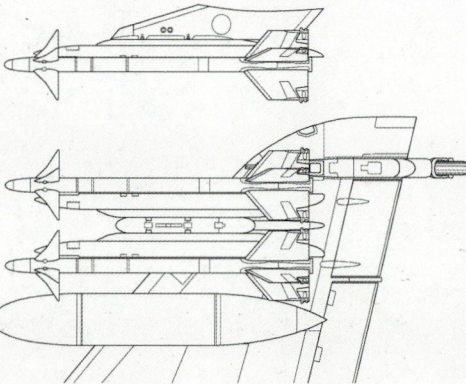

Matra R.550 Magic AAM
(outboard pylon; FRS Mk 51 only)

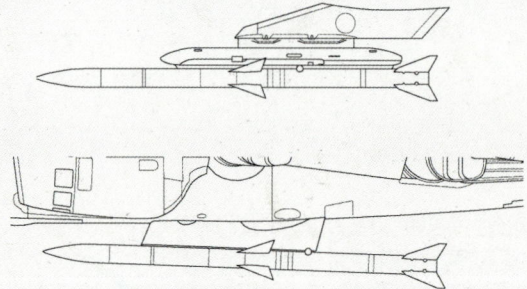

Sidewinder: twin mounting (outboard pylon; missiles
canted to clear stores on inboard pylon)

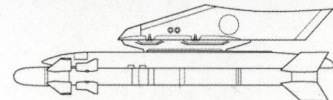

AMRAAM (FA Mk 2 only):
inboard (upper) and underbelly pylons

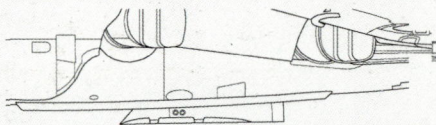

Centreline underbelly pylon
(could be fitted also when gun pods present)

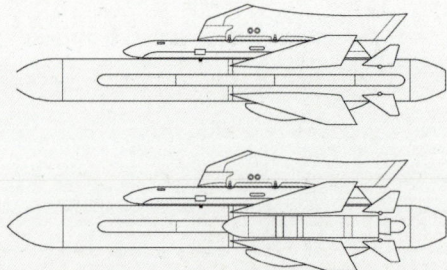

BAe Sea Eagle ASM (inboard pylon),
with additional booster rockets (lower)

Miscellaneous ordnance: 1,000lb GP bomb (top), Matra
pod for unguided rockets (above left) and CBLS (Carrier,
Bomb, Light Store) for practice sorties

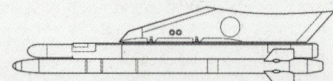

MBDA RAIDS (Rangeless Airborne Instrumented
Debriefing System) (outboard pylon; FA Mk 2 only)